Learn How to Sing

A Self-Help Guide to Teach Yourself to Sing

(How to Sing for Beginners)

by Rosslyn Michaels

Table of Contents

Introduction

Music is the most universal language in the world today. No other medium is able to bring us all together the way that music does. Ever since people invented the first flutes out of bones nearly 40,000 years ago and started to mimic those sounds with their voices, music has become ingrained into the human psyche. As interesting as this is, explaining how we learned these strange behaviors is not the objective of this book. Instead, our goal is to look into the art of singing and discover how to become better at it.

We must first define the concept of singing. It's basically the act of vocally holding a melodic note or a group of notes for a long period of time. A note is simply the pitch assigned to a sound that can be found on a musical keyboard as shown in the image below. Each octave begins and ends with the note "C".

Humans use a seven-note system with each note named after the letters A to G. All these notes have different sounds. As you ascend, you will find that some notes are merely higher-pitched versions of previous notes. That's why if you look on a piano, you won't just see seven keys. A standard piano starts with an A key all the way at the bottom, goes to G, then repeats this pattern throughout the keyboard. This is the case only for the white piano keys though as the black keys follow a different set of rules. The black keys have the names of the white keys that are closest to them; the only difference is that they are either "flat" or "sharp" depending on their position relative to a white key. For instance, if you look on the keyboard above and look at the A key, you will see that there is a black key to the left and another to the right of it. The black key to the left of A is called A flat (A♭), and the black key to the right of A is called A sharp (A♯). There are about 88 keys total on a standard piano.

When we sing a note, it will always correspond to either one of the black or white keys on the piano. Unfortunately, the human voice doesn't have the full range of a piano as our voices can only go so low or so high. Our voices are still very versatile though. Humans have the most versatile voices in the animal kingdom. In fact, humans are the only animals capable of deliberately holding a note for long periods of time. Yes, birds sing, in a way, but mostly as a form of communication. Humans, on the other hand, are able to manipulate, contort, structure, and change the way they sound when singing. With our voices, we are able to bring joy to ourselves and others while also communicating messages.

In this book, we'll discuss the different techniques that a beginner will need to know to start their journey to becoming a singer. Becoming a good singer doesn't happen overnight; you will need constant practice over a long period of time, and you will have to train your ears first before training your voice. Thus, most of the effort must come from you, and this guide is simply here to assist you while embarking upon the journey towards becoming a better singer.

Chapter 1: Identifying Your Vocal Range

Bass, tenor, alto and soprano — these are the four basic ranges of the human voice. Bass and tenor are usually attributed to the male human voice, while alto and soprano are attributed to the female human voice. The bass range is typically the deepest range of notes the male human voice can hit while the tenor range is the highest. Similarly, the alto range is the deepest range of notes the female voice can hit while the soprano range is the highest in the human vocal register.

Finding your range is not very hard actually; you can start by listening to the way you speak. Does your voice tremble when you speak? Do you have a sweet, squeaky voice? Do you have a mid-range or plain voice? Take a microphone or voice recording software and record yourself speaking. It may seem silly if you haven't done this before, and it will be certainly be strange if you're listening to yourself speak through a third-party for the first time. Your voice will sound oddly unfamiliar because what you hear in your head when you speak is not a true representation of what others actually hear; because when we speak, sound doesn't only come from our vocal cords.

The way we sound is heavily affected by our sinuses, nasal cavity, and our bones as well. Our sinuses and nasal cavity have lots of space where sound waves bounce around before they travel to the recipient's ear. However, it's not that the sound produced due to our sinuses and bone structure alters the sound that escapes our bodies that much. It doesn't. Rather, when we speak, we're hearing the vibrations happening in our bones, in our nasal cavity, and in our sinuses. This is why our voices sound so different when we listen to a recording, and it's also why you can't really trust what you hear on a regular basis to judge your singing voice. Chances are your real voice has less boom and bass, so keep this in mind when trying to find your range.

After recording and listening for your voice range, let's analyze the pitch and the timbre. Pitch is how high or low a sound is, while timbre is the distinctiveness or character of the sound. To further understand the concept of pitch and timbre, notice that hardly any two singers sound exactly alike. For example, Rihanna doesn't sound like Beyonce; Andrea Bocelli's sound is distinct from Luciano Pavarotti; and Whitney Houston doesn't sound like Mariah Carey. We all have something that makes the tone of our voices distinct. Your range can heavily depend on this. You may have a high sounding voice, but your timbre may show that you could be more of an alto than a soprano. It's all about listening and analyzing your own distinctive qualities.

Now that we have an idea how our voices sound when we speak, it's time to listen to how we sound when we sing. This may be tricky if you're doing this for the first time. You may need to utilize an instrument, so feel free to ask a guitarist or pianist friend of yours to help. You could also use a basic song, like "Mary Had a Little Lamb." Almost everyone can sing a tune like that, even if it doesn't sound too good. Record yourself and listen to the playback. Did you have a propensity to go lower in the song? Or were you more comfortable with the higher notes? Listen to all of that when figuring out your range.

To make a more accurate assessment, however, you will need the help of a musical instrument like a guitar or a piano. Ask a friend to play a "middle C" note, which is the C-note towards the center of the piano, also known as "C4" (see the diagram below). Try to repeat the exact sound that you hear. This will also help in training your ear. Aim to sing as close as possible to the note that you hear. The objective of this current exercise is not to be spot on, but to see how low or how high you can go. After middle C, move down the scale. If you can go below C3 (3 octaves lower), then most likely you are a bass. If you stop around C3, and you're able to go up above middle C all the way to E4, then you are more likely a tenor. If you are able to go further beyond E4 to an octave above that, then you are most likely an alto. If you're able to go above that, then you're a soprano.

All these types can be divided even further into subtypes. The different types of basses are namely basso profundo (contrabass), bass, and baritone. They depend heavily on the pitch of your vocal register. Contrabasses are able to go to G1 and probably even lower – they are able to reach the lowest ends of the human register. There are tenors and there are countertenors. Countertenors have the highest range for the male vocal register and can sometimes go as high as a soprano in strong and clear falsetto. Altos are divided into contralto and alto. Contraltos have the lowest range for the female vocal register and can go as low as a tenor or sometimes as low as a baritone. On the other hand, altos are able to hit the bottom of the soprano range. Sopranos, on the other hand, are divided into mezzo-soprano, soprano, and sopranino. Mezzo-sopranos have the lowest of the soprano range and can go up to around G5, sopranos can sing up to a C6, while sopraninos can go beyond that. Singing at the highest and lowest end of the musical scale takes skill and innate talent — and it is very rare to find either.

Don't worry about determining your subtype right now. Once you have found your primary range, it's time to get to work.

Chapter 2: Intro to Musical Scales

A musical scale is a succession of musical notes that increases or decreases by pitch. The "Do-Re-Mi-Fa-So-La-Ti-Do" we all learned in kindergarten or on *Sesame Street* or *The Sound of Music* is actually a musical scale. Try singing it in your head. This scale mimics the major scale. We won't go into much detail about what makes it a major scale, but it is necessary to know that music is built from these scales. "Do-Re-Mi" can be recited in a number of different keys. Think of a key as the note you start on in the scale, so if you start on the middle C note of the keyboard, then you are singing a scale in the key of C.

Ask a friend who has a piano to help you with practicing how to sing a scale. Learning how to sing a scale is an important fundamental of music and singing. Professionals practice scales all the time, not only with their voice, but with instruments as well. Reciting scales helps you warm up your voice before a performance and trains your ears. This is especially important if you consider yourself a tone-deaf person. As mentioned before, "Do-Re-Mi" is a major scale, and it usually consists of seven unique notes. Once you get more advanced, you will learn more about other scales such as the minor scale. Major scales seem happy and fun, while minor scales sound mysterious and sad. Many of our modern R&B and pop songs are in the minor scale. You will easily hear the difference if you ask your pianist friend to play a major scale and minor scale.

Before you start practicing your first scale, tell your partner on the piano or guitar to play the C major scale several times so you can hear it in your head. Listening to it repeatedly will ensure that you get it right. By this time, you should already know your range, so be sure that you start on the right C or you can run the risk of going too high or too low. If you are a tenor or bass, a safe bet is to start on C3, while altos or sopranos are advised to start on C4 or middle C. Once you have listened to the scale a few times and can hear it clearly in your head, it is time to attempt singing it.

Listen to the first note being played. Don't move on to the next note until you have the first note down pat. Proceed until you have reached the highest note, which should be C again. Congratulations, you have just sung your first musical scale!

When singing your scales, be careful not to go too fast so as to avoid doing them improperly or singing the notes incorrectly. It is better to sing one note ten times and get it right, rather than to sing the whole scale incorrectly ten times. You need to train your ear, and you can't do that if you aren't listening and repeating the correct note properly. As such, repetition is important: If you have a problem hitting the first notes of the scale, don't move on until you're able to hit it successfully. Yes, it can get old really quickly, but again, it's better to do it right than do it wrong. If you are struggling, ask your friend to play the scale over and over again and try simply listening along without singing. After listening to it several more times, then try singing it again.

After a few days or weeks, you should be able to sing "Do-Re-Mi" without the use of a keyboard in both ascending and descending order. Sing along in different keys (starting with A instead of C, for example), and you could substitute and sing "La-La-La" or something else instead of singing "Do-Re-Mi".

Chapter 3: Learning Breath Control

Professional singers are often able to sing scales that span several octaves. Some of them can even do this with one breath, despite the fact that singing the simple scale is hard enough in one breath. Singers learn to do this through breathing techniques to ply their trade. If they don't, then they risk sounding awkward constantly taking quick short breaths between phrases and words. Breathing in itself isn't hard; we all know how to breathe. When it comes to singing, however, it is all about control, and not all of us possess that skill. While you don't really have to think when you are breathing naturally; singing, on the other hand, requires that you tell your brain when it's appropriate to inhale and exhale. This is why breath training is very important.

In the words of Robert C. White:

"In the Beginning there was Breath, and Singing was with Breath, and Breath was Singing, and Singing was Breath. And all singing was made by the Breath, and without Breath was not any Singing made that was made."

One common theme is seen in this albeit humorous passage: You can't have singing without breath. Singing is actually exhaling while vibrating your vocal chords. It's possible to

17

breathe without singing, but it's impossible to sing without breathing.

Posture:

First, your posture must be taken into account. Posture dictates how much space will be available for air to fill in your lungs. If you are not standing or sitting properly, you will not be able to practice breathing properly.

When sitting, ensure that your back is straight. Do not lean back in the chair and don't slouch either. It is best to sit in the middle of the chair when singing. Place your feet flat on the ground with your hands either resting on your lap or holding the sheet music. If you are holding sheet music, have it leveled with your chin and no lower than your chest. It should be in front of you and far enough away that you will be able to read the notes and words. Having your music on your lap will hinder sufficient breathing since your head is tilted down.

When you are standing, ensure that you stand up straight and that your feet are flat on the floor. Your chest should be pushed out a little as well, as if you are feeling proud of yourself. If you are holding sheet music, follow the same guidelines as if you were sitting. If you don't have sheet music, keep your hands on your sides. Do not cross your arms against your chest or anywhere in front or behind you.

Inhalations:

Without inhalation, it would be impossible to exhale, right? The trick is to find the right number of times to inhale while singing. Sometimes inhalation has to be extremely quick, while at other times, singers have more than enough time in a song to rest and take in air.

A good singer knows how to take in enough air to finish a passage. It is necessary to learn how to inhale enough air in a fraction of a second to be able to sing a passage that lasts for several seconds or longer. When inhaling, you must get the air into your belly and not let it rest in your chest or else you won't find the space to sing when needed. Of course, the air is not really going to your belly, but it should feel that way because your diaphragm, the muscle that controls the cavity below your lungs, is moving downward to make space for your lungs to expand. The more you let your diaphragm move downward, the more air you are able take in.

Now try this very slowly. Take your time and pause between inhaling and then exhaling. Practice taking five-second inhalations, five-second breaks (holding your breath), and five-second exhalations. Then start decreasing the time for inhaling and increase the time for breaks or exhaling. Afterwards, start decreasing the amount of time for your breaks and vary the times in which you do each. When you breathe, make sure that you are pushing out your belly, not your chest. Your chest should actually be the last thing to stretch when inhaling. Your diaphragm can stretch much farther than your chest can, allowing you take in more air.

Exhalations:

Now it's time to start practicing exhalations. One good exercise professional singers practice is forced exhalations. This is done by trying to get all the air out in your lungs through unconventional methods. Perhaps you've seen people rumble their lips as a singing exercise?

If you don't know what that is, it sounds like a loud motorcycle or airplane, and you can do it by sticking your lips out like a duck, but softly without flexing. Then push air out through them. Rumbling your lips only lets as little air to go through as possible, thus this helps in sustaining exhalation. Practicing this sustained exhalation exercise will, over time, enable you to sing those high notes and long phrases. This is what a singer aims to do while singing: use as little air as possible to get the clearest note out.

Another such exercise involves practicing with a feather or leaf while standing or lying flat on your back: Place the feather on your lips and blow as hard as you can to try and get the feather as high as possible for as long as possible. Be sure to hold one end with your fingertips.

Chapter 4: Improving your Diction for Singing

Unless you're making use of wordless melodies, pronunciation is very important in singing. Some people put diction last on the list of things they need to practice when it comes to singing because they believe diction is only important for public speakers. However, if you are trying to convey a message through song, it will be lost if your audience can't understand you. This is why diction is so important.

Listen to any song — pop, classical, jazz, country, any genre you fancy — and you will find that you are able to understand all the words even when sung softly. However, sometimes when you listen to these artists performing the same song live, it's a different story. It's very easy to get lost in the music, but words are just as important in a song. To be able to speak through your music, you need to be understood at all times. And to do this, you need to practice diction exercises.

For diction, you should use the same exercises that public speakers do. Start with simple exercises and practice the most important thing in singing words: forming vowels. People often speak differently than they sing, so don't expect pronunciations to be the same. Pronouncing your vowels properly will ensure the message remains the same.

23

Diphthongs are two vowels sounds pronounced in one syllable, like in "lane" or "hour". In the case of diphthongs, when we speak, we follow the rule "the first one does the talking, the second keeps on walking." However, when we sing, both vowels are often pronounced. We sometimes transform even simple vowels into diphthong to accommodate their corresponding notes. Take the vowel "i" for example. Say the vowel over and over in your head. What do you hear? You will most likely hear the combination of two other vowels, "a(h)" and "e(e)." This is how we pronounce our vowels in music. Let's practice how we would form our vowels while singing a simple phrase. Let's sing, "I am in love with you." Don't mind the melody yet; we'll just try to focus on how we sing this phrase. When you are singing this phrase, it should sound something like this: "*Aeeh am een louv weeth yuu.*"

When we sing words, we're basically singing vowels enveloped by consonants. To visualize, let's think of a written letter. When we get a letter, do we pay attention to the envelope? No, but the envelope is important in delivering a letter. It's the same with consonants – we shouldn't put emphasis on them, but they are still very important. We form our consonants with our lips, teeth, and tongue. When you sing and you need to sustain a word, we prolong the vowel, not the consonant. "Been," when prolonged for example, should be sung as "*beeeeeen*" not "*beennnnnnn*".

When you are practicing your diction, concentrate on your tongue and how you use it. Allow it to move about as it needs. Recite as many tongue twisters as you can. Another way to practice your diction is through recording yourself and listening back to it. A better thing to do is to play it to someone else. If they can't hear all the words that you are saying, then you need to keep practicing. Finally, listen to great orators. Sure, they aren't singing, but listen to how they form their words. Some of them follow the same rules that singers do.

Chapter 5: Adding Vibrato

Vibrato is the vibration you hear when someone is singing, especially when they are singing longer notes. To a beginner, this is probably the trickiest technique to master. However, when you have mastered it and can perform it effortlessly, you are on your way to becoming a great singer. It is possible to do it badly, though, which can spoil the flow and feel of your song. A bad vibrato is a terrible thing to hear, so practicing how to do your vibrato properly is important.

First, open the back of your throat. Some people try to sing vibrato with a closed throat, but it doesn't work that way. If you don't really know what opening the back of your throat should feel like, try yawning. Feel and understand the mechanisms that are going on in your throat and mouth to take in and release all that air. Next, relax yourself completely, including your chest and stomach. A lot of people try and do vibrato with a tense stomach, which results in a forced vibrato that is obvious even to a toddler. Ensure that your posture is good and you are breathing properly, making use of the guidelines from Chapter 3.

Now that your body is set, you are ready to start practicing and singing the proper way. If you have been practicing by singing from your throat, STOP! It has been implied before in this guide but we'll say it more clearly here: The air you use to produce notes should always feel like it's coming from your diaphragm. Now sing one note — maybe start with a "Laaa." Again, remember that it should feel like it's coming from your lungs, not from your throat. Be sure the note is at a favorable pitch and try again. Keep doing it again and again, only then attempting to add the vibrato. It will come quite naturally to you, but don't be disappointed if you can't sing a clear vibrato right away. Just a little vibrato is progress. It's a good reminder not to force it. Not only does a forced vibrato sound terrible, but you could also hurt yourself. A good vibrato is always natural and subtle.

Vibrato is not for every song or every measure though. Vibrato is actually a rapid fluctuation in pitch, and if you do too much, you could fall in pitch. Vibrato is good to help add emphasis on passages, especially on longer ones. Hearing vibrato on short and quick words and passages sounds weird and forced. The only group that has been able to pull this off is Alvin and the Chipmunks, and we certainly don't want to sound like a novelty act.

There are times in certain types of music when you will need to exert a more forced type of vibrato. The vibrato in these cases helps to intensify a note or a phrase. You will often hear this at the end of show tunes, classical music, or jazz songs. However, in most cases, vibrato should always come naturally. Remember that subtlety is the mark of artistic beauty in music.

To help develop your vibrato naturally over time, try diaphragm exercises. Your diaphragm controls how well your vibrato is, so it helps to do breathing exercises to contract and relax your diaphragm. You can also do short breathing exercises in quick succession to achieve this. One more thing: while Whitney Houston is the quintessential example of a great singer, she did something that you should not practice doing — moving your jaw up and down in quick succession to mimic the vibrato sound. Don't do this. Producing vibrato through your jaws is the incorrect way of singing.

Chapter 6: Singing and Your Attitude

If you want to be a good singer — a great singer even — then you will need something to keep you going: the right attitude. If you start with the wrong attitude, then you're not going to reach very far — and your voice won't either. If you feel like you can't sing very well, don't smile and repeat, "Oh, I can't sing," every time someone asks you to sing something. If you really want to be a good singer, and you are in the process of learning, then your response should be, "I'm not very good yet, but if you want, I can try something." Having that kind of positive attitude will keep you in the right frame of mind to continue learning and moving forward. Hence, the first attribute that you should work on is your confidence.

Confidence is the key to telling your brain that you're hungry to keep improving, even though you may not get things right away. Don't be overconfident or cocky of course, as that will prevent you from really reaching your true potential, which could destroy your chances of being a good singer. Behaving that way tells your mind that you have achieved your peak and you know it all already. So when you have that attitude, you actually cease learning. Nobody, not even professionals who make a living singing, should have that attitude. We are all still learning. Author Isaac Asimov, whose works were preponderant of modern science-fiction, said wisely *"We only truly stop learning once we die."*

Set high yet realistic expectations for yourself. If you are a bass, don't tell yourself that you will be Luciano Pavarotti in a year. You may be able to increase your range, but by the time you have done so, you also have to learn the other techniques to be able to pull off a complicated piece like "Nessu Dorma" effectively. If you're an alto, don't set an expectation to be able to sing those high notes in Mariah Carey's old songs. There's nothing wrong with aspiring to expand your range, but everyone's voice is different and unique. Some voices will be able to do what others cannot. With that said, it does help to set mini-goals for your singing lessons. These mini-goals could include mastering a scale or two, being able to exhale for more than 10 seconds with only 1-2 seconds of inhalation breath, or something that you can achieve in a short amount of time. From there, keep on building your skills, and you will realize that these mini-goals have transformed themselves cumulatively into big achievements.

Conclusion

Now you're ready to become a superstar! Well, almost. Reading a book and doing a few exercises in one day won't suddenly turn you into a professional. Even though Whitney Houston and Luciano Pavarotti sang in two different genres and styles, they each hit the top of their fields through long periods of hard work and consistent practice. They didn't arrive at success overnight; they had to do things such as practicing scales and breathing exercises even well throughout their professional careers. No one ever stops learning and rehearsing the basics. Mastering the basics now will provide you with a solid foundation for more advanced techniques in the vocal arts.

It can get tiresome at times, especially if you are well-advanced in your years and your habits, but nothing is impossible. Many singers started their trade early in life, some even right out of the crib. But there are plenty of others that started later in life and have become masters as well. Private lessons will help you reach your goal much faster than working by yourself, so if you can, continue your training with a private voice coach. Even if you don't plan to audition for the next "American Idol," "X Factor" or "The Voice," being able to sing is something that will bring great joy to you and those around you.

Finally, I'd like to thank you for purchasing this book! If you enjoyed it or found it helpful, I'd greatly appreciate it if you'd take a moment to leave a review on Amazon. Thank you!

Made in United States
Orlando, FL
30 January 2023

29230087R00024